New Zealand

New Zealand consists of two large islands and a number of smaller ones nestled in the South Pacific. Roughly the size of Britain, Italy or Japan, it has a population of just over three million. Despite its geographical location, New Zealand is not an isolated country. While its roots lie in Europe, its branches of trade and cooperation are stretching out to the other major nations of the Pacific – Australia, Canada, Japan and the United States.

It is a land of two peoples – Maoris and Europeans. Together they have succeeded in building a modern state seemingly devoid of the problems of pollution, racial conflict and overpopulation which burden most other western nations.

In *We live in New Zealand*, a cross section of the people of New Zealand tell you what their life is like – life in agriculture, life in industry, life in the cities and life in the country.

The author, John Ball, is a freelance accountant and writer. He has traveled extensively throughout New Zealand and now lives in Auckland, North Island.

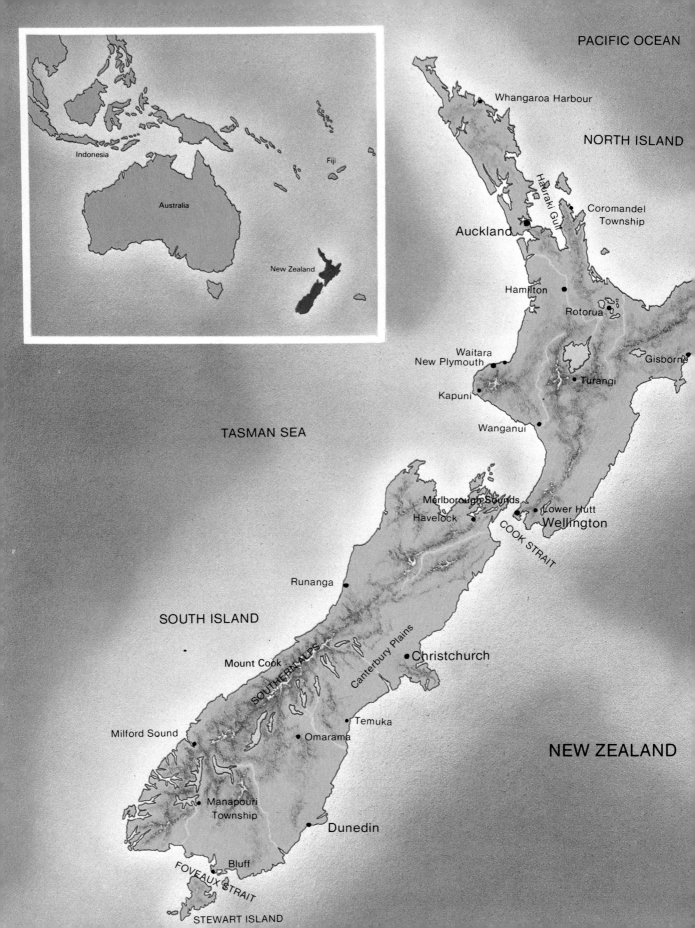

PACIFIC OCEAN

NORTH ISLAND

Whangaroa Harbour

Hauraki Gulf

Coromandel Township

Auckland

Hamilton

Rotorua

Waitara
New Plymouth

Gisborne

Kapuni

Turangi

TASMAN SEA

Wanganui

Marlborough Sounds

Lower Hutt

Havelock

Wellington

COOK STRAIT

Runanga

SOUTH ISLAND

Christchurch

Mount Cook

Canterbury Plains

SOUTHERN ALPS

Milford Sound

Temuka

NEW ZEALAND

Omarama

Manapouri Township

Dunedin

Bluff

FOVEAUX STRAIT

STEWART ISLAND

Indonesia

Fiji

Australia

New Zealand

we live in
NEW ZEALAND

John Ball

Photography by
Chris Fairclough

A Living Here Book

The Bookwright Press
New York · 1984

Living Here

First published in the United States in 1984 by
The Bookwright Press, 387 Park Avenue South,
New York NY 10016

First published in 1982 by
Wayland (Publishers) Limited, England

© Copyright 1982 Wayland (Publishers) Ltd.

ISBN: 0–531–04781–4

Library of Congress Catalog Card Number: 83–72805

Printed by G. Canale & C.S.p.A., Turin, Italy

Contents

"There are 73 million sheep in New Zealand"

Matthew Parsons is a shepherd at Birchwood Station, near Omarama. Birchwood is in the high country in central South Island. Born in the area, Matthew has lived and worked on high country farms all his life.

Up here on the edge of the Southern Alps is the only place you will find merinos now. This breed of sheep used to dominate the South Island stations, but with the arrival of refrigerated shipping there was a change to breeds which would produce good meat as well as wool. Merinos are really only wool producers, but they are useful here because they can feed right up to the snowline without needing supplementary feed or wintering indoors.

A shepherd's life can be a lonely one, but Matthew enjoys the isolation.

Birchwood Station covers 9,000 hectares (22,000 acres). We run 6,500 merinos. Most of the station is mountain country, so we rely on our dogs for herding and mustering (rounding up). A lot goes into the breeding and training of farm dogs. A well-trained dog can have amazing control over a large flock of sheep, and will guide them in response to commands from his owner.

Once a year, in December, it's shearing time. Gangs of contract shearers arrive, living on the station and working long hours each day. This job is one of the few remaining really hard jobs in farming, and there are many characters and legends amongst the shearers.

The wool is mostly sold by auction, $945,000,000 worth a year. 90 percent of this is exported to over fifty different countries. The marketing is controlled by the Wool Board, who maintain a minimum floor price by bidding themselves or supplementing the price to the farmer. This guarantees a return to the farmers and gives them confidence to develop their farms.

There are 73 million sheep on the 30,000 sheep farms in New Zealand. A typical farm will be run by the owner and his family. It will carry 1,500 ewes and produce 5.5 kg (12 lb) of wool per sheep. The lambing percentage will be close to 100 percent; that is, they will get one lamb for each ewe each year. Some ewes will have twins, which helps keep the numbers up. The New Zealand economy has in past years fluctuated with the world demand for wool. The current fashion trend towards better quality clothing and natural fibers is helping support the wool price at present. Competition from man-made fibers, which are much cheaper, has always been a problem, but a lot of effort is put into wool promotion world-wide.

A close second to wool is the meat production from sheep. Of the forty million lambs produced each year, twenty seven million are processed as "New Zealand lamb," which has a world-wide reputation for quality and flavor. Including mutton (sheep meat) and beef we produce 1,150,000 tonnes (1,265,000 tons) of meat a year, and consume 30 percent of it ourselves. This puts us amongst the biggest meat eaters in the world. Most of the sheep that are destined for meat production are first fattened on finishing farms on the coastal plains and river valleys.

These lowland farms are more compact, greener and easier to work than the high country stations. It's a different sort of farming, one that wouldn't suit me. I would miss the high hills, and the isolation. Most days I work on my own, with just the dogs for company. I never feel lonely; the country is too big and open. I have always enjoyed being on my own, which helps a lot in a job like this.

New Zealand is famous for its lush green pastures and for its lamb, which is exported to countries all around the world.

"My name is Maori for 'priestess'"

Ruahine Smith is fourteen. She lives with her family in Dunedin, a city of 120,000 people, on the southeast corner of the South Island. She attends secondary school and hopes eventually to be a policewoman.

Dunedin was first settled by people from Scotland, so many of the streets and suburbs now have Scottish names. In 1860 there was a gold rush, and the town grew very quickly into a wealthy merchant city. Now much of the industry has moved north to where there are more people, and these days Dunedin is better known for its medical university.

The weather this far south is not as nice as in the north. We get a lot of rain and cold winds, and in winter we get ice and some snow. It is fun for ice-skating and skiing, but you have to dress warm.

In summer it's a different story. The temperature gets up to 25°C (77°F), and it seems the whole town goes to the beach. The best one is St Kilda's, near where we live. It is a very good beach for surfing, so we see lots of board riders enjoying the waves. Most days we walk down for a swim after school. My brother Terry wants a surfboard, but he is only ten, and Mum says that's too young.

I go to school at the Moreau College for girls. It's a Catholic school. Our whole family are Catholics. Most state schools have boys and girls in the same class, but Catholics have their own schools, usually different ones for boys and girls. This is my fourth year at

Ruahine bites into her favorite food — hamburger and chips from a "take-away."

secondary school. Before this I went to primary school from when I was five until I was ten. Everyone in New Zealand has to stay at school until they are fifteen, but I want to stay until I am seventeen. Then, if I pass all my exams, I will be able to go to university.

At school I study religion, English, mathematics, science, social studies, home economics, art and sewing. For sport we play basketball, netball, volleyball and cricket. I am in the school cricket team, and sometimes on Saturdays we play against girls' teams from other schools.

When I leave school I want to be a policewoman. You have to be 1.65m (5ft 5in) tall and it takes two years' training and probation. I'm tall for my age, so I guess I will grow high enough. You don't join up until you are nineteen, so I want to go to university for a few years first. Then I can finish my degree while I am on probation. I will be able to get a better job and more pay in the police force if I have a qualification (degree).

My father is a builder. He was born in Ireland, and lived there until he left school. He came to New Zealand and married Mum, who is a Maori from Northland. That's how I got the name Ruahine, which is Maori for priestess. Mum was brought up in the Maori ways, and sometimes on weekends we all go on long trips to collect *kina* (sea-urchins), *paua* and *tua-tuas* (types of shellfish). Mum knows where to find them and how to cook them. My favorite is *pipis*, a small white shellfish which we collect from the beaches near home. You get them at low tide, just under the sand. You can fill a bucket in a few minutes. We steam them open and eat them straight from the shell, the way Maoris have for centuries.

When Mum doesn't feel like cooking, we buy our dinner from a "take-away" shop. There are lots of "take-aways" in New Zealand, and they all sell hamburgers (my favorite), hot potato chips and milk shakes. Some also sell fish, sausages, toasted sandwiches and other things. They are put in paper bags, and you usually eat them in your car or just on the street outside.

I have never lived anywhere else but Dunedin. I have been to the North Island on holidays, and I still like it here best.

Ruahine and her friends collect pipis *from the beach at St Kilda.*

"Our rocky shores have claimed many ships"

Ken and Dianne Gullery live in Havelock, a small town at the north end of the South Island. They operate the charter vessel *Glenmore*, which delivers mail to the many isolated communities throughout the Marlborough Sounds.

Before settling in Havelock I worked as a marine engineer on large ships. I enjoyed the travel, but I always felt my roots were here in the Marlborough Sounds, where I was born. My father was a whaler, one of the last participants in what is now a bygone era. I would sit fascinated, listening for hours to his tales of chasing the giant whales which were common around the New Zealand coast.

The whalers have all gone, but new industries have come to replace them.

The Marlborough Sounds consist of hundreds of kilometers of inland waterways and small islands, full of bush-clad mountains and sandy coves. Most of these are only accessible by sea, and their natural beauty is just being discovered by tourists.

The sheltered inlets have also seen the birth of mussel farming. The green-lipped mussels are grown on long

The Marlborough Sounds are flanked by green, bush-clad mountains.

lengths of rope suspended in the water from buoys. The shellfish take around fifteen months to reach their full size of ten cm (four inches) long. Several processing factories offer employment to local people, sorting and packing the mussels for export to the U.S.A., Australia, and Japan. The industry is just two years old, but already there are 180 farms of three hectares (seven acres) each, producing a total of 15,000 tonnes (16,500 tons) annually.

As well as the mussel farmers, there are sheep farmers, retired people, holiday cottages, and even a commune amongst the many secluded inlets and islands. The only access is by water, and each weekday I make a mail run in the *Glenmore* to a different part of the Sounds. The Havelock Post Office sorts the mail into individual sealed canvas bags. The delivery runs are very popular with tourists and holiday-makers, and for the residents our weekly call is often their only contact with the outside world.

At weekends we operate a dive charter service. Scuba diving is becoming very popular in New Zealand, as it is already in many other parts of the world. An amazing array of underwater equipment is now available, from air compressors to sophisticated underwater movie-cameras.

Although we do not have coral reefs, New Zealand has a wide variety of sea life, from colorful sponges to huge kingfish, as well as the much prized crayfish (similar to lobster). Our rocky shores have claimed many ships over the years, and a visit to a wreck site is always a popular part of our charter.

We can take up to ten divers at a time, and experience has shown us that good diving spots and good home cooking is a winning combination with most enthusiasts. Meals on board include fresh fish and crayfish caught during the cruise, but a lot of the other meals are prepared by my wife, Dianne, before we leave port.

Dianne has a very full-time job in Havelock operating the tearooms, which are open seven days a week. Once we are more established we plan to sell the tearooms, and then Dianne will assist me on the *Glenmore*.

Getting a new business established in a new area is a long, hard battle, but we have faith in the enormous potential of the Marlborough Sounds, both for new industries and for recreation and tourism. It is particularly rewarding for me to be a part of the growth of the area in which I was raised. Changing times have brought changing needs to the Sounds, and we feel that we are part of a new wave of pioneers.

While Ken is out on the Sounds, his wife runs the Havelock Tearooms back on shore.

"A tangi is a very moving experience"

Peter Waldron was born in Wellington. His mother was English, his father a Maori. He was raised on a *Marae*, and indoctrinated in traditional Maori values. Peter now lives in South Auckland with his wife, Sonia. They are both Maori wardens.

The Maori warden movement evolved from a desire to promote law and order within the Maori community in a way that was acceptable to their culture. It was also part of a repeated effort by Maoris to control their own destiny. Our Maori society has traditionally been a communal one, with authority being exercised by the tribal elders. Offenders were dealt with by people who knew and cared for them, and were respected by them. Maori wardens are not policemen. The only power they have is the respect, called *Mana*, that their community has for them. It is a voluntary job, but it is considered a great honor to be elected as a warden. We work within our community to promote law and order by treating the causes of disorder, rather than by disciplining offenders.

There are 290,000 Maoris in New Zealand. Over the years most have settled in the cities. The Maori word for white man is *Pakeha*. Our furniture and houses are of *Pakeha* design, but the Maori values are retained within our homes. We place great importance on family ties, including those with our ancestors who have passed on. We are much closer to the earth and nature than our *Pakeha* counterparts. Different families have traditionally held special skills, as orators, healers, or planters. These skills are handed down through generations, and held with great pride by the families.

The place where Maoris feel their culture the strongest is on a *Marae*. Each

Peter greets an old friend in the traditional Maori way, known as hongi.

community has its own *Marae* – an area of land containing a meeting house. A *Marae* is a sacred place; there are many traditions to be observed by locals and visitors, but there is also a strong sense of belonging for all Maoris. Some *Maraes* are simple buildings, others richly decorated with carvings. The traditions are more important than the surroundings. *Maraes* are used for meetings, weddings and all social occasions, but priority is always given to a *Tangi*.

We believe that when one of our people dies, their spirit rests in the body for three days before making the journey to their spiritual homeland. During this time the person lies in rest at the *Marae*, and is kept company by loved ones. It's a time for grieving, but it's also a time to express many other emotions, to tell stories, and to come to terms with the loss. A *Tangi* is a very moving experience; it brings out our feelings as

Maoris, and as a community of caring people; it is our way of saying goodbye to a loved one, within our own traditions and culture. Many people will stay for the three days, living at the *Marae*. Banquets will be prepared for these guests, often cooked in a *hangi*. The food is wrapped in leaves and buried in the ground on hot stones. Nothing tastes quite as good as meat and vegetables from a *hangi*.

Our children have grown up now, and we have nine grandchildren. We all live and work in a *Pakeha* world. The old Maori lifestyle was doomed by the onslaught of the *Pakeha* technology, but Maoris are becoming more and more aware of the spiritual values of their culture. They see that these values can be transplanted into a *Pakeha* environment. There is a regeneration of Maoridom, which is being seen in a more positive light by both Maori and *Pakeha*. I see our culture as playing an increasingly important role in New Zealand society in future years.

Peter shares a joke with some Maori friends outside their Marae, or meeting house.

"Milk is delivered to every house every day"

David Howie is 15. He lives with his parents in Wilton, a suburb of Wellington. He is a pupil at St Patrick's College in Wellington. After school David works for a milk vendor as a delivery boy.

I'm in the fifth form at St Patrick's College, which means that this year I sit my School Certificate exams, the first of the national exams. All fifth formers throughout New Zealand sit the same exams on the same day, and the results are scaled to give the same pass rate as previous years. English is compulsory, but I am also sitting for mathematics, science, accounting and technical drawing. If I pass School Certificate, next year I will sit a university entrance

When he has finished his schooling David hopes to study at one of New Zealand's six universities.

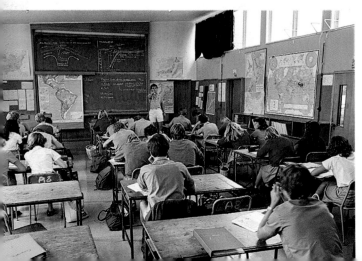

exam, which I must pass before I can be admitted to university. If I miss either I can go back for another year and try again. At university I hope to do a commerce degree so I can become an accountant.

The best part of school is the sports. I play cricket in summer and rugby football in the winter. We have our long summer holidays from late December to early February – usually six to seven weeks. I spend a lot of my holidays with my grandparents who live at Lake Ohau in the middle of the South Island.

After school I work for our local milk vendor. Milk is delivered to every house every day in the cities and towns of New Zealand. This is made possible by the town milk-supply scheme which nationalizes profits and prices. Dairy farmers are paid a flat fifteen cents per liter (about 12 U.S. cents a quart) for milk from their farms. Milk tankers truck it to the local treatment plants where it is pasteurized, bottled and sold to the vendors. The government subsidizes the industry, and sees that everyone gets a daily delivery.

Milk costs 25 cents (20 U.S. cents) for 600 ml (one pint). The bottles are all re-used, so the house owner puts the right number of empty bottles at their gate. Inside the empties they drop plastic tokens which they buy from the vendor. The tokens pay for the milk; we just replace empties with full ones. We also deliver cream, yogurt and fruit juices, which are sold in the same way.

It takes 2½ hours to do our round — four of us running with carts while the vendor drives the truck. Wellington is very hilly, so I run up and down a lot of steps where the cart cannot go. It keeps me fit for sport. We are paid $7 ($5.30 U.S.) a night; not a lot, but it's nice to have some money of our own.

At the end of my day I like to watch some TV. There are two TV channels in New Zealand, both color, both state operated. Everybody complains about the programs, but I think there are some good ones. We get a lot of "Coronation Street" and "Dallas" type programs, but we also get a lot of good documentaries, local and overseas. Our teacher often tells us to watch out for a certain current affairs or feature program because it's on a subject we are studying.

A milk bottling plant. New Zealand's milk industry is subsidized by the government.

"Our whole town is just one big family"

Ruth Hendley is 51 and the wife of a coal miner. She lives in Runanga, a small town on the west coast of the South Island. This part of New Zealand is known for its rugged coastline and high rainfall.

In our home there is a fire going all year round. Jimmy, my husband, says a house is not a home without a fire. It gives a warm, cozy feeling to the living room. We get a lot of rain here, about 300 cm (118 in) a year, so a fire helps keep the damp out too. Our daughter, Lynette, lives with us. At eighteen she would probably have "gone flatting" (rented an apartment) if we lived in the city, but in Runanga families stay together much more.

In a small New Zealand town, everybody knows everyone else.

Both Jimmy and I were born in Runanga. We know everybody in the town; it is like one big family. We have many friendships which go back to when we were toddlers. I couldn't imagine moving to anywhere else; it would be like trying to start life all over again.

Jimmy has been a miner for thirty years. Coal mining is the traditional industry of the west coast. Most of the miners work in the big state mines, but Jimmy and four of his mates operate a private mine on leased land. They have to design and build all their own equipment. They start at seven a.m. and work until they fill their agreed quota, about 40 tonnes (44 tons). West coast coal is mostly used in industry and homes in New Zealand, but some is sold to Japan.

After work they all go to the workingman's club for a few beers. Jimmy usually gets home around five p.m., by which time I have our dinner almost ready. We usually have steak or lamb roast. Meat costs around $4 a kilo ($1.40 U.S. a pound), but fish is much

The rugged west coast of South Island lies open to the prevailing winds.

cheaper. We also eat a lot of vegetables, mostly grown from our own garden.

During the day I like to attend meetings at the women's institute, or at one of the church groups. We talk about the needs of our community, organize fund-raising social events, and enjoy each other's company.

On Saturday it's the races. Horse racing is said to be one of New Zealand's national pastimes. The state-operated betting agency turns over $500,000,000 ($380,000,000 U.S.) a year. We all have to be quiet while Jimmy listens to the race commentaries on the radio. I occasionally have a bet, but I never seem to win much.

Jimmy owns shares in a racehorse, and sometimes we go to Christchurch to watch it race. As it's a four-hour drive through the pass over the Southern Alps, we usually stay overnight in a hotel. I don't often get a chance to shop in the city, so I enjoy hunting for bargains while Jimmy talks with the trainers. However, it's always nice to get back to our beautiful west coast.

In New Zealand the government takes responsibility for a lot of the people's needs. It is often called a "welfare state." For example, there is national super-annuation. Everybody over sixty is paid 80 percent of the average weekly wage. It costs about $10 to visit a doctor, but all prescribed medicines and public hospitals are free. There is also the accident compensation commission. All employers pay a levy (tax), and if any worker is injured while at work the commission pays all of his medical expenses and most of his wages while he is off sick. This saves a lot of worry and hardship for the families involved.

None of these benefits existed when we were children: life was much harder for our parents. Still they seemed to enjoy themselves just as much as people do today. I think as long as you have your family and friends around you, that's the main thing.

"Bluff oysters never have pearls in them"

Walter Fowler is 30 years old and an oysterman at Bluff, at the southern tip of the South Island. He works in the family business, along with his father, three brothers and sister.

Two hundred years ago whalers and sealers used to fish these waters. A hundred years later the first European settlers came and joined the native Maoris. The settlers soon discovered the Bluff oysters, now renowned for their strong flavor and large size.

The Bluff oystermen have to venture out into the Foveaux Strait in all weathers.

In those days they could be collected inshore in shallow water, but now we need to go much farther out. We dredge for them in the middle of the Foveaux Strait, which separates the South Island from Stewart Island. The oysters lie amongst the sand and shingle on the sea bed.

Foveaux Strait, like Cook Strait at the other end of the South Island, is known for its rough weather. The winds funnel around the bottom of the Southern Alps and combine with the strong tides to make steep waves which are dangerous to small boats. We are in the "Roaring Forties" wind belt, so storms and cold weather are common.

To operate in these waters the boats must be strong and seaworthy. Our vessel, the *Miro*, is one of the original sailing scows which were common around the New Zealand coast, and is a veteran of many storms. In her trading days she would anchor inshore at high tide, then load and unload while grounded by the falling tide.

The industry is carefully controlled to preserve the oyster stock. The 23 vessels presently licensed are limited to 5,000 sacks each per season. Each sackful weighs 79 kg (174 lb) and holds between 55 and 70 dozen oysters.

We head out to sea before dawn and start dredging at first light. The hardest work is the "culching," which is separating the oysters from all the other bits of sediment. Shells less than five cm (two inches) across must also be separated and returned. It is often cold and wet, but on a good day we can fill 60 sacks. The crew are paid by the sackful, so they work very hard.

Back at port the oyster shells are opened by hand and the flesh either canned or deep-frozen. They sell for around $3 a dozen from Bluff, but in a restaurant you would pay a lot more. As the catch is limited, they are all sold within New Zealand, but overseas visitors often make a point of buying a few cans to take home.

We can only dredge during the winter months, because the oysters spawn during spring and summer. When we can't dredge for oysters we trawl for fish and do the maintenance work on the boats.

Unfortunately, Bluff oysters never have pearls in them, but there are still a lot of rewards in being an oysterman. I enjoy working with my father and brothers, and of course there are always plenty of oysters to go round. We never get tired of that special flavor.

Walter unties the Miro *in harbor at Bluff and sets out for a day's oyster dredging.*

"The biggest backyard in the world"

Roger Bird is the controller at the Manapouri hydroelectric power station. He is married and has two children. He has a degree in electrical engineering and a great love of the outdoors.

I have been working on hydroelectric power stations for ten years now. Manapouri is my fourth station, and by far the most interesting. I live with my family at the works village at Manapouri Township. The station is on the far side of Lake Manapouri in the South Island. There is no road access, so my day starts with a one hour scenic launch trip around the lake edge.

From my desk I have a sweeping view of the lake and mountains. My job is to co-

The machine hall at the Manapouri hydroelectric power station is open to the public.

ordinate the activities of the 61 employees, and to monitor the machinery. The turbines and generators are 213 meters (700 feet) underground, in a huge hall excavated out of the rock. The waters of the lake drop down vertical shafts, through the turbines, then out along a ten-km (six-mile) tailrace tunnel to the coast.

In New Zealand we have a few power stations which burn coal or use geothermal power (power derived from heat in the interior of the earth), but 87 percent of our electricity comes from hydro stations. Our fast flowing rivers and steep sided valleys make ideal sites. Usually a large dam is constructed, and an artificial lake created behind it. Electricity cannot be stored: it must be generated when it is needed. Without a lake to act as a reservoir, there would be no generation during the dry spells. At Manapouri there is no dam needed, because the lake is already 177 meters (580 feet) above sea level.

All New Zealand's power stations are open to the public. I think this one is the most exciting. Access to the machine hall is by bus, via a long tunnel which loops down inside the mountain. The hall itself is most impressive. The hewn granite walls contrast with the modern machinery. Each of the seven huge turbines has an output of 147,000 horsepower, and generates 100,000 kilowatts of electricity.

On my days off I take the family tramping (hiking). Manapouri may be a small town, but it has an incredibly big backyard. Fjordland National Park, covering 1,212,000 hectares (3,000,000 acres), is one of the largest in the world. Many parts are still unexplored, and the beauty of the virgin forests, lakes and mountains is endless. One of the unique things about the New Zealand bush is that there are no dangerous animals. In fact there are no "furry four-legged animals" other than a few introduced ones. Instead, we have flightless birds like the Kiwi, the emblem of New Zealand.

All the sheep, horses, cows, deer, dogs, cats and rats in New Zealand were initially introduced by the white man. Conservationists are concerned at the damage these animals do to the native bush and to the birds. For this reason a lot of effort is being made to establish endangered species on the offshore islands, where access can be controlled.

Camping with a small tent is our children's idea of a perfect holiday. For me it provides a chance to spend time with my family and enjoy the outdoors. The power station feels huge when I am working there, but against the backdrop of the lake and mountains, it's really just a small dot.

Roger travels to work by launch as there are no roads to the power station.

"We are five hours from the nearest city"

Yvonne Methley is 21. She works at the T.H.C. Hotel at Milford Sound, in the south of the South Island. The Sound is 200 km (125 miles) off the main road, via a winding pass through the mountains.

Up until a few years ago I was a bank clerk in Auckland, where my family live. My boyfriend was working as a management trainee for the Tourist Hotel Corporation (T.H.C.). When he was transferred to the Milford Hotel I applied for a job there so we could be together. At first I missed the busy city, with its shops and theaters. The change in the climate also came as a shock

Mitre Peak, the symbol of Milford, dominates the view from many of the Milford Hotel windows.

to me, but the isolation was the hardest thing to get used to.

The staff here are a cheerful group. I work both at the reception desk and in the souvenir shop, so I deal with the guests a lot, which makes my job more interesting. Most of us work a six-day week. We are 2½ hours' driving from Te Anau, the nearest town, and five hours from the nearest city. With only one day a week off there isn't really time to go anywhere, so we just enjoy the activities around the hotel.

A lot of the staff are into tramping (hiking). The hotel is in Fjordland National Park, so there are lots of good tracks. I'm a fairly "indoors" sort of person. I prefer knitting and sewing. In Auckland I enjoyed going to the beach to swim and sunbathe, but here the water is too cold, and it's always raining. We get an incredible 620 cm (244 inches) a year, the highest rainfall in New Zealand.

In sounds like a strange place to have a hotel, but there is a lot to see and do at Milford Sound.

The T.H.C. is a state-owned organization that specializes in opening first-class hotels in isolated places which have a lot of scenic beauty, so as to encourage tourism. The T.H.C. hotels all have "silver service" restaurants and top facilities. Most of our guests are from America, Australia or Japan, but of course we get a sprinkling from all over the world, and quite a few New Zealanders too. They all come to see the Milford Sound, with its mountains and waterfalls. The best way is on a scenic launch trip.

The Sound is a long narrow strip of very deep water with mountains on each side. It is 14 km (8½ miles) from the top end, where the hotel is, to the ocean. The launches cruise the length of the Sound, often escorted by dolphins and seals. Chicken and champagne lunches are served, and the launches make stops at the foot of the big waterfalls. The Sutherland Falls are the most famous; they have a sheer drop of 580 meters (1,900 feet). After heavy rain they are really spectacular, and at Milford, rain is something you can rely on.

Between showers you get a glimpse of Mitre Peak, the symbol of Milford. All this rain does make you appreciate the sun when it comes out. When it shines on a still day, you get the most perfect mirror reflections on the surface of the Sound. The mountains have snow on their tops most of the year, and they really are very beautiful.

The staff all feel the isolation, and this seems to bring us together. We have parties regularly, and they're always lots of fun. In a few months my boyfriend is due for another transfer, and I will be going with him. I will miss the people here. I have made many good friends. I will miss the beautiful Sound, and in a funny way I will even miss all that rain!

The Milford Hotel is set among some of the most dramatic scenery in all New Zealand.

"The whole industry operates on cooperatives"

Bruce Selbie is a dairy farmer in Temuka, on the fertile Canterbury Plains. He has a diploma in agriculture from Lincoln College, New Zealand's agricultural university. Bruce's farm produces milk for town supply, and breeds calves for beef cattle farms.

Our family have been working dairy farms in this area since 1925. We have 130 Friesian cows on our 120 hectares (300 acres). Irrigation is our biggest problem. The soil is fertile, but here on the eastern side of the Alps we have a very low rainfall. We have plenty of water available from artesian wells, but spreading it around the farm still takes five hours a day during the summer. We use a large pump and a mobile sprinkler line, which has to be moved progressively across the pastures.

During the spring growth we make hay and silage for the winter feed. On most

The motorcycle is now more widely used than the horse on New Zealand's dairy farms.

New Zealand farms this is sufficient, but because of our dry climate we grow a barley crop to supplement the hay.

We milk cows early in the morning. Around mid-morning the milk tanker comes and collects the day's production. We farm our land very intensively, and as a result get 5,700 liters (9,150 pints) of milk per cow per year, which puts us in the top 30 yields in the country.

Our farm is a partnership between my brother and me. We also employ another hand, which brings us in line with the national average. Of the 153,000 farm workers in the country, two-thirds are owners or members of the owner's family.

Motorcycles have all but completely replaced the horse as a means of transport on New Zealand farms. For us it is now an essential piece of equipment; it's very fast and mobile so we rarely walk anywhere. Most farmers also become very attached to their bikes, and will discuss the merits of different models for hours. Initially we used sports bikes, but now there are specially designed farm bikes, which are

New Zealand cheddar being made at one of the largest cheese factories in the world.

more rugged, and will even tow trailers.

All of the milk from the farm goes to town supply, which means it is pasteurized and bottled for consumption in the home. About one-third of the country's milk production is processed into dairy products such as butter, cheese and milk powders. One of the unique aspects of dairy farming in New Zealand is that all the processing and marketing of the products is owned and controlled by the farmers. The dairy factories are cooperatives, owned in proportion to the amount of product each farmer supplies. The marketing of the products is controlled by a board which employs experts, but whose directors are elected from amongst the farmers. Even the milking equipment on our farm was developed and built by a farmers' cooperative.

There are around three million dairy cows in New Zealand. They feed on pastures all year round which makes the butter we produce very yellow in color. As a nation we eat more butter per head than any other country. Strangely we eat very little cheese, although we produce 105,000 tonnes (115,500 tons) a year, mostly for export. Ten years ago Britain took 75 percent of our cheese exports, but since joining the Common Market she takes only 9 percent.

Most of the dairy calves are sold to be raised as beef cattle. There are five million beef cattle being raised for meat production. Once again it is an export orientated industry, with by far the biggest customer being North America. I personally much prefer eating beef to lamb, but very few New Zealanders would agree with me. Roast lamb is the traditional meal.

"Lots of trees and open spaces"

Jane Holton-Jeffries was born in England. Her family emigrated to New Zealand when she was three years old, 21 years ago. She, and her husband, Wayne, both work as bus operators in Christchurch, South Island.

Christchurch city could be called a real bus drivers' paradise — a warm climate, wide, tree-lined streets, and friendly people. Being on the Canterbury Plains, the land is flat, which is most unusual for a New Zealand city. Wellington is built on the mountainside; Auckland nestles amongst scores of volcanic hills; and even Dunedin is hilly.

Here in Christchurch we have 295,000 people, which is one-third of the population of the South Island. It's a nice size for a city: big enough to be busy, but small enough to be friendly. To the west, the Southern Alps protect the city from harsh weather, so we get many hours of sunshine with just 600 mm (24 in) of rain per year. Trees and flowers abound and Christchurch is known as the "garden city" of New Zealand.

On the east coast there is Lyttleton Harbour, with good boating and sheltered swimming, and also New Brighton beach, where people can surf in the Pacific Ocean.

Our red buses run on scenic tours to the coast, but most of our passengers are commuters traveling to and from work. There are no underground trains in New Zealand and, except in Wellington, suburban rail links are scarce. In spite of this, most bus companies are losing customers and having trouble meeting their operating costs, as private cars are by far the most popular means of commuting. Private bus companies cannot survive, so local authorities usually provide bus services which are subsidized by taxes from ratepayers (tax payers).

The Christchurch Transport Board has a modern fleet of 187 buses, and employs 300 operators, of whom 25 are women. I was one of the first female operators, and initially the passengers were as nervous of me as I was of them, but we soon got used to each other.

The buses are very easy to drive, and it only takes a few weeks to get a license. Being an operator means you collect the fares as people board. There are no conductors, so it's like having two jobs at once: driving the bus and dealing with the public.

My husband, Wayne, is also a bus operator. We drive different routes, but we both work the same shifts. Sitting in a bus all day is not a good way to keep your figure, so for exercise we both cycle the five km (three miles) to work and back. We both get the same pay, around $5.50 ($4.20 U.S.) per hour, and we work as much overtime as possible, as we are saving to buy a house.

Some mornings we have to start at five a.m., which is the only part of the job I don't like. The best shift is four p.m. to midnight, as we have all day to swim at the beach or to ride our horses.

Horses are our main interest outside work. We own four at present, but our new house will come with four hectares (ten acres) of land, so we will be able to breed and sell them. The house and land will cost from $70,000 to $100,000 ($53,200 to $76,000 U.S.) but we only need a quarter of this as a deposit. We will both need to work to pay it off, but we don't mind this because we both love bus driving, and it leaves us with plenty of time for the horses.

In Christchurch, passengers can hook their empty baby carriages onto the front of the bus.

Most of the buses in New Zealand are run by local authorities and subsidized by taxes.

"My life revolves around cars and driving"

Glyn Clements is a 23-year-old traffic officer with the Ministry of Transport in Wellington City. He is married and lives in Lower Hutt, a city just fifteen km (nine miles) around the harbor shore from Wellington. Glyn's hobby is vintage cars and motorcycles.

It's a warm sunny day. I'm on the motorway patrol, cruising around Wellington's foreshore. The harbor is sparkling. I can't imagine a more pleasant job. I'm a traffic officer with the Ministry of Transport, Road Transport Division. The main objective of the division is to "promote the safe and efficient use of the roads." To help achieve this it employs almost 1,000 of us traffic officers throughout the whole of New Zealand.

We are not policemen, and have only limited powers of arrest, but we are a trained and uniformed enforcement agency, who specialize in transport law. We have a close liaison with the police force. As traffic officers we enforce all the laws to do with road transport. We patrol

The traffic control room in Wellington is the nerve center of the city's Road Transport Division.

streets to see that the rules of the road are complied with; we issue drivers' licenses, and we see that all vehicles are road-worthy.

To become a traffic officer you must have attained a reasonable level in education, be between nineteen and thirty years of age, be at least 1.73 m (5 feet 8 inches) tall and in good health. If accepted you do a three-month live-in course at our training college, followed by a twelve-month probationary period. We are trained in transport law, high-speed driving and vehicle handling, first aid, and detention psychology.

We use motorcycles a lot, because they are quicker in traffic, and we use radar speed detectors to check motorists' speeds. The maximum allowed on motorways is 80 km per hour (50 miles per hour); in cities 50 km per hour (30 miles per hour). If a motorist is exceeding the limit we can issue an offense notice. The driver can then either pay the prescribed fine or go to court to defend the charge.

Traffic officers work very hard at maintaining a good public image. If we are on motorway patrol and we see a car stopped on the roadside, we will pull over and offer assistance, get the vehicle going if possible, or use our radio to contact a mechanic or a tow truck. We consider this an important part of the job, as public co-operation is essential to making the roads safer.

We also attend and investigate accidents, and where necessary check drivers for alcohol levels. We have powers of arrest where drunk-driving is involved. I often wish these drivers who have little regard for road safety could see the results of accidents that their behavior can cause.

My life revolves around cars and driving. I love vintage cars and motor-cycles. Restoring an old motorcycle can keep me happy for hours.

New Zealand is a very car-minded country. We have over two million motor vehicles, that's more than one for every two people. They are mostly imported as parts, and assembled here. We assemble cars from Japan, Australia and Britain. We also import assembled cars from Europe and many other parts of the world. It all goes to make up the biggest selection of production model vehicles per head of population anywhere in the world.

Petrol (gas) is costly in New Zealand, so small economical cars are most popular. You can get a drivers' license once you turn fifteen, and most young people want a car or motorcycle soon after that. The car is the number-one status symbol in New Zealand. For many people it is also a necessity, as cities are sprawled over a large area and public transport is limited.

Glyn cruises along a highway in Wellington to discourage motorists from breaking traffic laws.

"Being a painter is a bit like being a reporter"

58-year-old Hans Brutsch was born in Switzerland. At the age of 23 he came to New Zealand to farm. He is now a landscape artist working from Auckland, where he lives with his wife, Fay, and their two daughters.

I have found a lot of happiness in painting. A painting should communicate something of the artist's emotions, and should be an enjoyable experience, both for the artist and the viewer. Children seem to understand this better than adults – their paintings are always joyful and happy. Too many artists are serious and dramatic these days.

I started painting when I was forty. I thought that if I just produced pictures I would soon get bored, so I took up learning

Hans is a slow, meticulous painter, but he still manages to make a living from his skills.

to paint rather than painting. Instead of taking lessons, I worked out techniques for myself. It gave me a lot of satisfaction, even though it was a bit like reinventing the wheel.

Now I paint between four and eight hours every day. My paintings are not just landscapes; they are interpretations of the land. It takes a lot of concentration to get the feeling onto the canvas. All my paintings are sold to art shops and I get around $350 ($265 U.S.) each for them. I am a slow painter, but I still do reasonably well out of it, which is a bit of a problem really. People seem to like artists who either are poor or who make millions. They seem suspicious of anyone in between.

New Zealand is a strange place for arts and culture. The people are very "culturally aware" – there are a lot of amateur and professional theaters, an opera and ballet society, and a renowned symphony orchestra. All these are supported by sponsors and by the public. But for the performers, a career in the arts is very difficult, because in New Zealand there just aren't enough people to support them. The country produces more than its fair share of international standard performers, but they soon find themselves looking to Australia, Britain, or the United States of America for bigger audiences and more recognition.

For painters it's a lot easier – we don't rely on audiences for our income. Most of my paintings are of rural scenes, especially the rolling hills of the Northland farms, where I worked before becoming a painter. People often say my paintings have a special feel about them. I think this is because I know the land from seventeen years of working on it.

The beautiful, empty landscape of New Zealand would inspire any artist.

Now I see farming through a painter's eyes, and I feel concerned for the land. Some farmers are clearing all of the bush to make more grasslands. If they left patches of native bush on the steeper slopes they would help preserve nature's balance. The bush would also retain moisture during the rain, and would reduce soil erosion, a major problem in the north. I am sure they would get more production in the long run. Northland is also seeing lots of pine forests being planted. They should be planting native forests too, even though they take much longer to grow. We should be thinking more of future generations.

Being a painter is a bit like being a reporter, except you don't have to be impartial. You can enjoy putting your own opinions onto the canvas.

"My home is a one-room cabin"

Russell Sanderson is 20 years old. He was born and raised in Auckland, but now enjoys working as a bushman in the forests in the far north of New Zealand's North Island.

My home is a one-room cabin on the edge of Whangaroa harbor. The locals will assure you it is the most beautiful harbor in the world, and watching the sun set on a summer's night it would be hard to argue with them. It's 4 km (2½ miles) from Kaeo, the nearest town, and the rent for the cabin is just $25 ($19 U.S.) a week. It's isolated, but I love the quiet and the independence.

I work for the New Zealand Forest Service as a bushman. From seven a.m. to four p.m., Monday to Friday, I clear the scrub which grows around newly planted seedlings, or prune young trees to make them grow straight and tall. For this I'm

Much of New Zealand's farmland is now being replanted with pine trees which are used for commercial purposes.

paid $160 ($120 U.S.) per week after taxes. The work is hard, but I love the outdoor life.

At present I'm working in the Otangaroa forest, which, like nearly all of New Zealand's commercial forests, is a man-made forest of pine trees. These trees were first introduced from California, U.S.A., during the Depression of the 1930s, when thousands of men were employed by the government to plant seedlings. This gave birth to what is today a major industry, with 387,000 hectares (950,000 acres) planted, producing 8.6 million cubic meters (300 million cubic feet) of timber a year.

The trees I work on are usually only a few years old and about three meters (ten feet) tall, but over twenty years they will grow to 30 meters (100 feet). Then they will be cut down, and new seedlings planted in their place.

Before the white man arrived, the land was covered by dense native forest, dominated by the giant kauri trees, much prized by the English as masts for their ships. The small areas of kauri forests remaining are now protected, with the forestry industry concentrating almost exclusively on pine trees.

We work in gangs of five or six, sometimes hiking for hours deep into the forest to work on a new section. We take cut lunches, usually sandwiches, fruit and cake, and every few hours we take a short break to enjoy a cup of tea. As fires are totally prohibited in the forest we always have a large Thermos to keep the tea hot.

About half of the pine timber goes to Japan, where it is used in low-grade construction. The rest is used in New Zealand in the manufacture of paper, and in building. The output is increasing every year, and new markets are always being sought. In New Zealand the pine is used extensively to build houses and furniture, but it is not favored by overseas manufacturers, as it is a light-colored timber with darker knots at regular intervals. Local manufacturers have learned to use this to their advantage and make a feature of the knots.

By the end of the present century, timber production will have trebled, which will mean lots of work for people like me. There will always be a good market for the timber, but better prices are obtained when it is used in products like furniture, rather than when it is processed for paper, plywood, and other products.

On weekends I like nothing better than getting out on the harbor with a few friends. There is excellent fishing and swimming within a stone's throw of my little cabin.

The pine wood is used in New Zealand for furniture and house building.

John Ball and Chris Fairclough regret to announce that shortly after this interview was conducted, Russell Sanderson was tragically killed while at work in the New Zealand bush.

33

"As city farmers we have the best of both worlds"

Carol Wareham was born and raised on a farm in the country. She now lives with her husband, Gordon, and their two teenage children on a small farm on the outskirts of Auckland.

Gordon, my husband, was raised in the city. He is a fireman and wanted to continue his career after we were married, which meant we had to live close to the city. I had lived on a farm all my life and couldn't imagine any other life, nor could I think of a better environment to raise children in, with lots of animals, and room to grow. So we did what many New Zealand couples do: we bought a small farm close to the city.

In New Zealand it is common for the land around the cities to be divided into lots of between 4 and 10 hectares (10 and 2 acres). There are many thousands of these lots, or "farmlets," with many different uses, such as deer farming, breeding horses or cattle, cultivating citrus orchards growing nut trees, kiwifruit, vines flowers or market gardening (growing vegetables for local markets). Some owners even choose to leave their property covered with native bush, to enjoy the natural surroundings. Some of the more intensive farms on good land are very profitable, but most are like ours: they can earn enough to cover the costs of owning them, but you must have a regular job to support the family. Owners of these farms are called "city farmers."

As city farmers I feel we have the best of both worlds. Gordon is just 30 minutes by motorway from the Auckland Central Fire Station, where he works. We are close

Some city farmers prefer to leave the land around their farms in its natural state.

enough to the city to enjoy its amenities, yet we can also enjoy the country life.

When the children were younger we used to market-garden our land. We grew silverbeet (spinach), sweet corn, cauliflower and pumpkins, as well as some root crops such as carrots, turnips and kumera – a type of sweet potato much loved by New Zealanders. In those days I worked very hard in the fields. The children would help after school, and at harvest time we would employ extra labor.

I enjoyed it very much, but it was very hard work, and our farm was not really sheltered enough, so we would sometimes

Carol Wareham and her family have turned their city farm over to horse breeding.

lose a crop in bad weather. Today we use the land to breed horses, which can be very worthwhile – providing you breed a champion! To help support the farm I now have an office job in the city. I work from 8:30 a.m. to 4:30 p.m. Monday to Friday, traveling to and from work by bus.

If our horse breeding is successful I will give up the job. I like to go to the city to shop, but I don't enjoy working there. A small farm like ours becomes something the whole family can get involved in and enjoy. On weekends we all participate in show-jumping events. Winning ribbons is an important part of horse breeding, and we take great pride in seeing our children and our horses do well.

"I'm in the business of helping people"

The Reverend Wilfred Ford shares a joint ministry with his wife, the Rev. Mary Ford, at St Paul's Church, in Hamilton Central. Mr Ford is 61 and was born in Christchurch. He has been a minister of the Methodist Church for 37 years.

As a parson, I'm in the business of helping people. Anyone can knock on my door, and I will do my best for them. They don't need to be a member of our church or of any religion. Jesus Christ helped all comers, and He is our model. We aim to make St Paul's a "Body of Christ." When Christ was on earth He had great influence on the people around Him. It's this influence, this human presence, that we aim to continue. Following Christ's example, we care for the body, mind, and spirit of people. We don't set out to convert people to our beliefs, but we do hope that our example will attract others.

I joined the ministry in 1945 after serving for some time in the army. Since then I have at various times been a director of Christian Education, chairman of the Marriage Guidance Council of New Zealand, and deputy chairman of the New Zealand Broadcasting Corporation. Life in the church can be adventuresome – I once represented the Council of Churches on a visit to the Vietnam War.

St Paul's lies right in the middle of Hamilton's business center. It is made of wood, as were most buildings constructed around the same time. With redevelopment of the city it now looks quaint and homely amongst its more modern neighbors. I think it's symbolic that it's the oldest remaining building in its area, for the church was amongst the first institutions established by the white man in New Zealand.

Right throughout the South Pacific Islands, missionaries were close behind the explorers. For most of the natives, the first white man they met was a minister. Not surprising that today Christianity has a strong following amongst Maoris and Islanders. The Samoan Island Methodist community here in Hamilton hold a weekly service in their native tongue. The Maoris have a religion called *Ratana*, which is based on the Bible, and has a strong following amongst their people.

Religion also came to New Zealand with the early settlers from Britain. Over 70 percent of the total New Zealand population now list themselves as belonging to one of

St Paul's Methodist Church in Hamilton, where the Reverend Ford is minister.

the traditional Christian churches. Despite this, practising Christianity is not all that popular at present, but I believe the tide is turning. Even if it were not popular, I would stick with it because I believe it is the answer, for us as individuals and as a community.

Traditional eastern religions have come with immigrants from these countries, but today newer eastern sects, like the Hare Krishna, are always represented at music festivals and other large gatherings of young people. Recent years have seen a growth in the American-based Christianities. The Latter Day Saints (Mormon) church in particular crusades strongly, and has built an impressive temple on the outskirts of Hamilton. These religions are more authoritarian than the traditional Christian churches. I feel this approach has a lot of appeal to people who find themselves in a free and easy world.

I am still strongly of the belief that religion should free me to model my life on Jesus Christ, and not restrict me in that endeavor. He set a perfect example for us to follow.

Wilfred and his wife stroll along Hamilton's main street, close to St Paul's Church.

"I wanted to be my own boss"

Murry Pope is the managing director of Sea Bee Air Ltd., a small airline operating amphibious planes in the Hauraki Gulf. The company employs fifteen staff in Auckland and five in the Pacific Islands.

Five years ago I was chief pilot for this company. The owners wanted to sell, and, like so many New Zealanders, I wanted to be my own boss and to have a chance to run things my way, so I bought the company. Running a business in New Zealand is not easy: you have a small market and a lot of government control. Like many other companies, we soon found ourselves looking to overseas markets to expand our operation and to benefit from the many tax

Passengers begin to board one of Murry's Grumman "Widgeon" seaplanes.

incentives offered to exporters.

These Grumman "Widgeon" seaplanes have been servicing the islands of the Hauraki Gulf since 1955. We run scheduled services to the more populated islands, and a charter service to the others. The aircraft are amphibious; they can land and take off on the sea. So we have no need for airports and can operate from the harbor in downtown Auckland direct to any part of any of the islands. Some 45,000 passengers a year fly by Sea Bee Air. We have our regular commuters who live on the islands and work in the city, but most of our passengers are tourists and holiday-makers, or island residents visiting the city. We also make a lot of ambulance trips, carrying everything from injured trampers (hikers) to pregnant ladies. There hasn't been a baby born on a plane yet, but we have had some very close calls!

Our company saw a need for a service like this amongst the many small islands north of Fiji. We established a base at the island of Funafuti, and now deliver freight and take passengers on social and medical

trips under contract to the Tuvalu government. As with the operation in Auckland, it has low overheads and is tightly controlled. We can never compromise on safety, but we work hard to keep our costs to a minimum. We just don't have enough passengers to support any fancy overheads.

Tight restraints of this kind are very common to New Zealand companies and are among the reasons why so many people leave for overseas, particularly to Australia, in search of better wages and conditions. Over the last five years we have had a net migration loss; that is, more people leaving permanently than arriving. It has reduced a lot now, but in 1979 it peaked at 40,200. A lot of these people were skilled tradesmen, particularly from the building industry, which is sensitive to changes in the economy. Many people feel that the absence of these skilled workers will make it much harder for the economy to recover.

I am very fond of New Zealand, and would be reluctant to leave. Like a lot of

Murry Pope's airline flies 45,000 passengers to the islands off New Zealand every year.

those who stay, I feel it's the lifestyle, not the livelihood, that keeps me. I was born in Dunedin and spent many years working down there. I was a deer hunter in the Fjordland National Park. I worked for a few years on the construction of Manapouri power station; then I qualified as a pilot. Aviation has been in my blood ever since. I was transferred to Auckland and fell in love with the Hauraki Gulf. I believe it would be the tourist spot of the South Pacific if the weather were more reliable in winter. Anyone who develops a tourist resort in the Gulf must be prepared for a very quiet off-season. Charter yachts are starting to become established, but compared to other countries the Gulf is in a very undeveloped state. A lot of the locals feel this is the major part of its charm, but it makes it hard for people like me who are running a business here. However, it is still a beautiful place to operate in and I feel I will be here for quite a few years yet.

"The fishing industry is poised for a big change"

Ian Strongman is 23 and was born in Coromandel, North Island. After leaving school he served his apprenticeship as a cabinet-maker, but he is now involved in commercial fishing with his father.

Coromandel was just a very steep-sided peninsula, unfit for farming and so overlooked by early settlers, until somebody discovered gold. That was over 100 years ago, but Coromandel Township still retains some of that gold-mining flavor. Old workings are common, and even now conservationists are battling with large

Ian checks his nets before setting out for a day's trawling.

mining corporations over what gold still remains.

It's a very beautiful part of the country – lots of native forest and sheltered harbors. There's lots of good fishing too, so when Dad suggested we work a fishing boat together, I had no hesitation in leaving my cabinet-making to join him.

Dad bought a 16-meter (52-foot) boat, built of Kauri timber, and set up to trawl for snapper. Traditionally fishing is not as steady an employment as cabinet-making – you are dependent on both good catches and good market prices. But the fishing industry in New Zealand is poised for a big change.

It all started in 1978 when the government declared a 322-km (200-mile) "Exclusive Economic Zone." This has not extended the country's territorial waters, but it does mean that New Zealand controls the conservation and management of all fish resources within 322 km (200 miles) of its coastline.

It's a big responsibility, and a lot of effort is put into learning more about the resources through scientific research. Quotas are allocated to local and overseas fishing vessels. The zone covers 3,300,000 sq km (1,300,000 sq miles), so policing is also a big job.

The government has been keen to see New Zealand benefit from offshore fishing, so it has encouraged "joint venture" schemes. An overseas country provides the vessel and the skills, while local companies provide crews and processing plants. Most of the catch is then exported back to the participating country. In this way we are learning new technology, and experiencing new methods, while they are gaining access to our fishing grounds. Fish being caught include tuna, shark, barracuda, squid and dozens of other species not caught commercially by us before. The New Zealand economy also gains from the export earnings, currently around $160,000,000 a year ($121,600,000 U.S.).

Dad and I are somewhere in the middle of this change. We still fish for snapper, but our catch is exported direct to Japan. Our boat is a trawler, which means we fish by towing a net along the sea bed. When it is full we winch it on board and empty the fish into the hold. The fish are then carefully packed down between layers of ice, to freeze and preserve them. We stop fishing when our supply of ice runs out, usually after three days. Then it's back to Coromandel to unload the catch and take on more ice.

All the processing is done on shore, so just Dad and I are needed on board. In accordance with tradition, as crew I get a quarter of the catch and pay a quarter of the food and fuel costs. The skipper provides the boat and takes the other three-quarters. We get about $70 ($53 U.S.) for a 40-kg (90-lb) basketful of fish. On a really good day we would fill 400 baskets. Last season I made $20,000 ($15,200 U.S.) – double what I'd earn as a cabinet-maker.

The fishing is seasonal, so when we are not fishing I enjoy restoring old cars, or just chatting with my mates in the pub. Long holidays are another thing that cabinet-makers don't get!

A good haul of red snapper fish waiting to be weighed and transported to market.

"Two of the mountains are active volcanoes"

Kerry Erutoe is married and has eight children. He is 43 and a Maori, born in Northland and now living in Turangi at the southern end of Lake Taupo. Kerry is a grader driver for the Ministry of Works in Turangi.

Many of the back roads of New Zealand are graveled, often because there just isn't enough traffic to justify the cost of sealing them. In the steeper country you find roads that are unsealed because there is a lot of landsliding and subsidence, and it's a lot easier to maintain a gravel road. The roads wouldn't last long if it weren't for us graders. After a few good storms or a lot of use, they wear into ridges and potholes. A couple of runs with the grader has them fixed as good as new.

Grading the roads around Turangi has been my job for the last eighteen years. In summer, when it's nice and warm, things are fairly quiet. By making an early start I can be finished by lunchtime, then get into

Many of the back roads in New Zealand are graveled. Kerry has to ensure they remain open in all weathers.

some trout fishing in the afternoon. In the streams around Lake Taupo we get rainbow and brown trout – the big ones are up around six kg (thirteen lb) and they taste beautiful. Plenty of good pig hunting around these parts too. It's not too hard to catch them as long as you have a good hunting dog. There used to be a lot of deer to hunt too, but they are getting scarce now. People hunt them from helicopters. They use tranquilizer guns so they can sell them live to the deer farms.

In winter it's a different story – lots of overtime for me keeping the road clear after storms; and lots of traffic too, as the skiers come from everywhere to the National Park. This central part of the North Island is on a high plateau, so we get plenty of snow and ice.

There are three very big mountains around Turangi. They are: Tongariro (1,968 meters – 6,500 feet), Ngauruhoe (2,291 meters – 7,500 feet) and Ruapehu (2,797 meters – 6,400 feet). Ruapehu has got lots of good skiing. On a good weekend there will be 30,000 people on its slopes. They have plenty of good facilities for them – the main lift for skiers goes almost to the top of the mountain.

Two of the mountains are active volcanoes. Ruapehu has a lake of hot water inside its crater and every few years we get a small eruption, with mud and ash being spread over the mountainside. Ngauruhoe is a bit more aggressive, probably because he is so young, being only about 2,500 years old (his brothers are about one million years old). He is smoking most of the time, and occasionally you can see a fire or hear a rumble from his crater.

These mountains are sacred to the Maori people, and we have many legends about their history and their powers. They were within the Tuwharetoa tribal land, and a great chief of that tribe, Te Heuheu Horonuku, arranged for them to be gifted to the state, to be preserved for future generations. The gift was accepted in 1887, and so New Zealand's first national park was formed.

This part of the country is rich in Maori history. It was here the Maoris made one of their last stands in the wars with the white man. Many Maoris today are bitter about the loss of their ancestral lands. I listen to the old people talking about the great warriors of the past, and I also hear our young people talk of land rights. It seems to me that land is behind most of the conflicts of mankind.

In winter, Kerry has a hard job to keep the roads passable for people going to the snowfields on Mount Ruapehu.

"Our parliamentary system is based on Westminster's"

Bob Bell is the Member of Parliament for the Gisborne electorate. He is married and has three adult children. Prior to being an M.P., Bob worked as a land valuer and a farm adviser, and he has always been closely involved with the farming community.

It's relatively easy to become a Member of Parliament in this country. You don't need any great wealth or influence, just the backing of a political party and of the voters in your area. Once elected you are the representative of the people in that area in Parliament, a very full-time job. I spend a lot of my time listening to their suggestions and channeling them to the right department, or using my influence on their behalf.

All M.P.s in New Zealand are very accessible to the public. A common method of contact is the telephone. I am

One of the fine homes being built by growers in the Gisborne area.

also available most days a week for personal appointments, and once a month on a talk-back radio program, where people can call anonymously to discuss any subject that concerns them.

This accessibility, and the long hours I work, mean that my family get involved in the job. My wife, Anne, often attends functions on my behalf, and acts as my private secretary when I am away. I am fortunate that my children have grown up. Members with young children face considerable extra pressure.

As well as my house in Gisborne, I also have an apartment in Wellington, the capital city. This is where the New Zealand Parliament sits and where I spend about one-half of my time, contributing to the governing of the country, and promoting the interests of my area and its people.

Our parliamentary system is based on Westminster's. We have 92 electorates (constituencies). There is a House of Representatives, but no Upper House. Elections are held every three years, and the minimum voting age is eighteen. Each electorate elects a member, who may either represent a political party or be an "independent." I belong to the National Party, who are currently the ruling party.

The area I represent has seen a lot of changes in recent years. We have been in the forefront of the move to diversify our land use, to meet the changing overseas demand, and to overcome hill-country erosion. In our case traditional hill-country sheep farms have been replaced with pine forests: while the maize and cannery crops on the flatlands are being replaced with a wide variety of horticulture. Kiwifruit, a berry about five cm (two inches) long with a brown, furry skin and a soft, green center, is a recent discovery as an export crop. Already export earnings are $60,000,000 ($45,600,000 U.S.). Grapes for white wine are grown extensively. Our top growers reap over 32 tonnes per hectare (14 tons per acre). Peaches, citrus fruits, avocados, and many others grow well in the rich soil.

These new crops have greatly increased land values. Farm incomes have also risen which has had a flow-over effect to the towns. A lot of this new wealth is reflected in the many large and beautiful homes constructed in recent years.

There is always an element of risk in trying new crops, but the growers combine the latest technology with lots of enthusiasm, and it is pleasing to see their efforts rewarded.

Bob used to be a farm adviser and he is always keen to discuss a problem with the farmers in his electorate.

"Maoris had no written language"

Emily Schuster lives with her husband in Whakarewarewa Village in Rotorua. She is a descendant of the Te Arawa tribe of Maoris. Emily works for the New Zealand Maori Arts and Crafts Institute, where she teaches traditional handicrafts.

I have always had a great love of Maori crafts, so when I was accepted as supervisor of women's handicrafts I felt both excited and honored. The institute was formed in 1966 by an Act of Parliament to help preserve the crafts of the Maori people. We provide displays and demonstrations for the public, but the most important work is our teaching. Maoris come from all over New Zealand to train as tutors.

The men come to the institute to learn how to carve. They are taught not just how to use a chisel but how to record emotions, legends and history in the intricate designs. Carving is our traditional way of recording events and honoring ancestors, as the Maoris had no written language.

The women come to learn how to make garments, baskets, floor mats, and many other items from the leaves of the flax bushes. Some are functional goods, such as baskets for collecting *pipis* from the beach, but others, like the feathered coats, are very intricate and beautiful, taking hundreds of hours to weave. These are prized possessions when completed. The tutors take their skills back to their homes and in turn teach other Maoris, so ensuring that the crafts will be kept alive.

The institute is supported by the 260,000 tourists who visit each year, and much effort is made to cater to their needs. The carving and weaving schools have been designed as working demonstrations of Maori art. There is also a large replica of a Maori *pa*, or fortified village, showing how we lived in pre-European times.

In A.D. 1350 there was a great migration across the Pacific by the Maori. Seven large canoes came to *Aotearoa* (later named New Zealand by the Europeans). The descendants form the seven tribes of Maoris that we know today. They each went to different parts of the land. My tribe, the Te Arawa, settled in central North Island. They were a warlike race, and many a bloody battle was fought between tribes and subtribes. The young warriors took much pride, which they called *mana*, in their bravery in battle. Most villages had a fortress, or *pa*, in

The Maori Arts and Crafts Institute helps to keep Maori traditions alive.

which people lived during battles. The *pa* was surrounded by palisading, from which it was defended.

Within the *pa* here at Whakarewarewa there are examples of storehouses and family dwellings of that period. The degree of the adornment around the doors and windows indicated the social position of the occupants. The focal point of the *pa* is the meeting house, a large hall richly decorated with carvings from the institute's graduates. Here, schools of learning are held, where the legends, songs, chants and rituals are handed on by experts to the younger generation.

The village in which we live is also open to the tourists. It is set in a geothermal valley. The paths to the houses weave around boiling mud pools. Steaming water trickles out of the ground from hundreds of small springs, while farther down the valley the spectacular geysers shoot boiling water 100 meters (330 feet) into the air.

As well as fascinating the visitors, all this geothermal activity is very useful for us residents. Much of our cooking is done in steam boxes, built above the hot springs. The food cooks beautifully, with no loss of moisture or flavor.

As is the tradition, we never do the cooking or washing inside our homes; so having nature provide communal facilities suits us ideally. Our own children are all married now, but my husband and I are still surrounded by treasures and mementoes handed down from our ancestors. In this way their presence adds a warm atmosphere to the home. At the end of a busy day of teaching and meeting tourists, my home is my retreat, where I feel relaxed and at peace with the world.

The valley where Emily lives is full of geysers and bubbling hot springs.

"Auckland is an ideal place for yachting"

Tony Barker is a doctor of medicine, and commodore of the Richmond Yacht Club. He is 37 and lives in Auckland with his wife, Chree, and their three children. On weekends the family like to go cruising on their ten-meter (33-foot) yacht, *Arwen*.

I discovered sailing when I was twelve. I learnt the traditional way through sailing dinghies and small yachts. In those days keelboats were block-and-tackle and hard labor. Now we have well-balanced boats with good winches. Our keelers are crewed by families instead of teams of keen young men. Small yachts still have a huge following, but more and more people are learning on the family keeler.

I was born in Auckland, but lived in Dunedin for nine years while I attended the medical university there. Each summer holiday I would come back to Auckland to go sailing. I am now employed at the

The marinas of Auckland are always packed with colorful yachts and cruisers.

Auckland Hospital as a clinical bio-chemist. I work nine to five, Monday to Friday, which leaves the weekends free.

Auckland is an ideal place for yachting. We have excellent facilities in the many clubs and marinas; the wind averages ten to fifteen knots, and rarely storms without warning, and we are just two hours' sailing time from empty beaches. Sail out of Auckland harbor and you are in the sheltered Hauraki Gulf, with lots of quiet bays and beautiful islands, most of which are reserves. The Hauraki Gulf Maritime Park contains over fifty islands, with a total area of 9,200 hectares (22,750 acres). These islands are preserved in their natural state for recreation. You are free to land and explore, or just enjoy the beaches. Some of the more isolated islands are wildlife sanctuaries where endangered native bird species have been re-established.

Because there are so many places to go we can plan our sailing to take advantage of the wind. Our eldest daughter, Louise, is ten and quite content at the helm, having been raised on a diet of sailing. Chree and I feel that yachting is an ideal family activity. The confines of the yacht bring us together, and the adventure and occasional discomfort of rough weather are a worth-while experience for the children. There is plenty of company amongst the other yachting families, and we often plan to meet up with friends at the end of a day's sailing. Swimming from the golden beaches in the late afternoon, cooking freshly caught fish on an open fire on the beach – this is our idea of how to spend a weekend.

As commodore of Richmond Yacht Club I am also involved in organizing yacht races. There are races most weekends for yachties who prefer the excitement of

New Zealand is fast making a name for itself in international yachting events.

competition. Our top races will attract a field of 500 keelers, spread over nine divisions. Competition is keen, and a large industry has developed to cater for racers' needs. Boatbuilders, sailmakers and ships' chandlers all compete to have the latest innovation or the best-quality product.

New Zealand is usually well represented at international yachting events, and we have had some encouraging successes in recent years. Our annual offshore races to the Pacific Islands are also popular, with 100 or more yachts entering. I enjoy the occasional race, especially the family cruising races, but for us the real enjoy-ment of yachting is using *Arwen* as a holiday home, where the family can enjoy being together, mobile, in the fresh air and close to the elements.

"The ferries provide a vital link between the islands"

John Oliver works on the ferries which take passengers and vehicles across Cook Strait between the North and South Islands. He is married and has three sons. While on duty he lives on the ferry, but his home is a farm just north of Wellington.

As second officer I am responsible for the loading and unloading of the vessel *Aratika*. We carry 800 passengers, 70 cars, and 50 railway wagons. The car and train decks are always full during the summer months, and it requires a lot of organizing to get them all off and the next load on within the one hour allowed. We believe it is the fastest turnaround of its type in the world.

There are four vessels in all operating across Cook Strait, making a total of 2,000 return trips a year. The ferries provide a vital link both for freight and for holiday-makers. New Zealand's two main islands are roughly the same size, but three-quarters of the population live in the North Island. Despite this, the South Islanders have always referred to themselves as the "mainlanders."

Our journey from the south end starts at Picton, deep within the sheltered Marlborough Sounds. The passengers enjoy the beautiful scenery of the narrow fjords while we chain down all the cars and rail wagons. After about one hour's steaming we come into Cook Strait itself, known as the "windpipe of the Pacific." The high mountains on each side cause the wind to funnel through the strait. The Cook Strait is just nineteen km (twelve miles) wide, but it has a reputation as a very treacherous piece of water, and claims many ships. The wind gusts to over 63 km per hour (40 m.p.h.) on 188 days of the year, and over 96 km per hour (60 m.p.h.) on 41 days on average. The weather is also very unpre-

The Aratika *sets sail into the Cook Straits – a most treacherous stretch of water.*

John checks that all the cars disembark safely from the Aratika.

dictable. I have often seen a light northerly breeze on a mild day change to a southerly gale and heavy rain within ten minutes!

Soon we round the headlands into Wellington harbor, with its sparkling waters and high green hillsides. All that wind does have the advantage of giving clear smogless skies and low humidity. It's an extremely beautiful harbor. As we complete our 96-km (60-mile) journey, the vehicles are unchained, and we get ready for the big rush again, unloading and reloading at Wellington.

The round trip takes 7 hours 40 minutes, including one hour in port. The vessels all have lots of lounges, bars, children's areas and even a discotheque. Many of our passengers do the round trip as a mini sea cruise, enjoying the spectacular scenery.

All the crew are members of the Seamen's Union. By an agreement negotiated with the employers we can compress our hours. I work from six a.m. to midnight for four days, and then I can take eight days off. A second officer earns around $25,000 ($19,000 U.S.) a year, but this can vary a lot with years of service and qualifications.

I spend my days off with my wife and our three sons on our farm. We have 1,300 sheep on our 120 hectares (300 acres), so there is always plenty to do. I take my annual holidays during the lambing season, when I need to be on the farm full-time. I really enjoy the complete change of lifestyle from ferry to farm.

"The ultimate challenge is to climb Mount Cook"

Gavin Wills is the senior alpine guide at Mount Cook National Park. He is also a geologist, ski instructor, and a pilot. He lives in Mount Cook Village with his wife and two children.

People have always been attracted to Mount Cook. It has an aura which is felt by everyone who visits it. The village is perched in a fold in the mountains, a mere dot against the sheer mass of Mount Cook, which is 3,764 meters (12,350 ft) high. Sunset on a clear day sets the mountain glowing soft pink and sends tourists scurrying for their cameras.

Skiplanes have skis under their wheels so that they can take off and land on ice.

The tourists arrive by aircraft or luxury coach. They enjoy the first-class facilities of the Hermitage Hotel, or the more economical comfort of the chalets. The first hotel here was opened in 1894, well before the advent of roads and public transport. But even then, the long and difficult trek by horseback did not deter guests from coming to Mount Cook.

The national parks are perhaps New Zealand's greatest asset. There are ten major parks throughout the country, covering a total area of 2,158,000 hectares (5,300,000 acres). Mount Cook National Park contains the highest part of the Southern Alps, a mountain range which runs right down the middle of the South Island. The park contains 140 peaks over 2,100 meters (6,890 ft) high. These mountains are very young geologically, being just six million years old.

Before that they were below sea level. Buckling and shifting of the large continental plate that New Zealand sits on forced the higher mountains above the surface. The area rose by about 15,000 meters

(50,000 feet), but the erosion wore the mountains down to their present height, and formed the plains on either side.

Glaciers have also left their distinctive mark on the landscape. Successive ice ages have caused them to advance and recede, cutting long narrow lakes and valleys and carving out coastal fjords. The Tasman Glacier stretches for 27 km (17 miles) down the mountainside.

In winter the glacier is covered with snow. You can ride in a skiplane to the top and have an exhilarating 13-km (8-mile) ride downhill. Skiplanes play an important role at Mount Cook. The fourteen aircraft take 40,000 people a year on sightseeing trips to the glacier. They also ferry in skiers, mountaineers and supplies to the less accessible parts of the mountains.

There are fourteen alpine guides employed at the park, providing guide services to mountaineers who come from all over the world. The ultimate challenge for most is to climb Mount Cook. The climb can be done in five days, but because of the unpredictable weather, it usually takes ten. The nights are spent in mountain huts or "bivi-ing" out on the snow in small tents. It is a trip for experienced mountaineers only, but there are many easier climbs. We run a mountaineering school, and for the non-climbers there are exhilarating raft rides down the rapids of the Tasman River.

These mountains have been my home, my work, and my passion for ten years, and still every day brings something new. Our work is dictated by the weather and dominated by the mountains. Although we see tens of thousands of visitors, isolation is our major problem. Yet nothing can match the sparkle we see in the eyes of a client who has just completed a long and difficult climb, or the bond of friendship that results.

The Tasman Glacier is a 27-km (17-mile) river of ice which runs down the Southern Alps in New Zealand's South Island.

"Half of the unemployed are under twenty"

Carol Banks is 29. Born in Wellington, she is a qualified teacher who was unable to find suitable work in her field. Carol now lives in Auckland and works on an Unemployment Relief Scheme.

There are 753,000 people in the Auckland area, where I live. This is over twice the population of any other New Zealand city. It has a very temperate climate, 2,140 hours of sunshine a year, and the temperature rarely goes outside the range of 5-24°C (41-77°F). There are wealthy areas with grand homes and poorer areas with lots of state rental housing. The city center has one main street, Queen Street, with a large pedestrian square between the end of the street and the harbor. Many new buildings are going up and many old ones are being restored. There are lots of big stores and small arcades. The shopping is good except on Sunday, when everything is closed. Like many places though it also has a high rate of unemployment, especially amongst the young people.

Unemployment has been around for a few years now. Politicians make policy statements, but it seems a shortage of jobs is something our society will have to learn to live with. Unemployment pay is $50 ($38 U.S.) a week for a person under twenty, and $65 ($50 U.S.) if you are over twenty. It pays the food and rent if you group-live, but the real problem for most people is having so much time on their hands. There are about 50,000 registered unemployed in New Zealand, that's four percent of the work force. Half of these are under twenty. About 37,000 more people are on relief

Carol with her many friends at the Youth Resources Centre in Auckland.

work, that's jobs which are created or subsidized by the government to relieve the unemployment problem. Amongst these jobs are new positions created by the private sector, large groups of workers planting trees and gardens for local councils, and people like me being employed to help other unemployed people.

The Youth Resource Centre, where I work, is one of the good things to come out of unemployment. The Centre was the dream of Ted Jones, a youth adviser with the Auckland City Council. Ted was particularly keen to help the "city kids," young people who live or spend most of their time in the inner city. The Resource Centre is located just off Queen Street, and provides a training center and a focal point for the city youth. The young people are paid a wage to attend at regular hours and receive training in a variety of skills. The teachers are all employed under relief schemes to provide the training. From this base the Centre has grown to meet the much broader needs of the young people.

Unemployed school leavers present special problems. After a few years of living on the benefit they can lose their basic work habits and their confidence, and are in danger of becoming unemployable. At the Centre they learn work-related skills like woodwork, carving and sewing, but they also learn the basic social skills like budgeting, banking, first aid and training for a drivers' license. With the help the Centre provides they gain confidence in their work and in their ability to learn.

A lot of support has been received from companies and individuals around Auckland. The Centre has grown to include secondary schools and other youth groups within its programs. A telephone counseling service called Youth-line operates 24 hours a day from the Centre.

Auckland town center. Auckland is the largest city in New Zealand, with a population of 753,000.

The result is that young people gain confidence and ability, for employment or for unemployment, which leads to a pride in themselves and a new direction in life.

Working at the Centre is the most enjoyable and satisfying job I have known. The atmosphere is warm and friendly, and there is a feeling of achievement about the place. It's good to feel something is being done to help these people, but if our society is going to continue to have a shortage of jobs, then we will need to re-think our values and our education system to take this into account.

"Immigrants all come to find work and a better life"

John Teiti was born in the Cook Islands, in the South Pacific. He emigrated to New Zealand when he was seventeen, in search of work. John is now 34, shares an apartment with friends, and works as a window assembler in Auckland.

When I first came to New Zealand I couldn't believe how cold it was. That was during autumn, so winter was still to come. After the tropics, where I had been until then, I couldn't imagine how people lived in this climate. However, like most of the immigrants from the Pacific Islands, one New Zealand winter and I was used to it. Now I really like the climate, and I enjoy the beaches and swimming more than I did in the Cook Islands. In the tropics you always seek shade, but in New Zealand you get out and enjoy the sun.

There are a lot of Pacific Islanders in New Zealand. The Cook Islands, Niue and Tokelau all used to be territorial islands of New Zealand before they were granted independence. The people from the islands are New Zealand citizens and have unrestricted right of entry. With better health facilities the populations of all the Pacific Islands have grown larger than the islands can support, so the immigrants all come to find work and a better life. There are 58,000 Polynesians in Auckland. No other city in the Pacific has this many.

There are also a lot of immigrants from other parts of the world, especially the United Kingdom and Australia. Most of these people apply for permanent residence under the Occupational Priority Scheme. The government lists occupational skills that New Zealand is short of, and people with those skills get priority. They must meet all the usual requirements as to health and good character, and so on.

There is also a scheme under which entrepreneurs can obtain permanent residence, so they can set up a business which will provide employment or export earnings. Under the United Nations Scheme, New Zealand accepts a lot of refugees from South East Asia. For large groups there is a reception center in Auckland where they live while on a six-week orientation course. At the factory where I work, a refugee from Vietnam is employed. When he first came he couldn't speak much English, but he learned fast and he is now "one of the boys."

All the immigration helps to make Auckland a multi-cultural city, and an

Karangahape Road, one of the Polynesian quarters of Auckland.

interesting place to live. New immigrants are coming from the islands all the time, and I enjoy showing them around. Auckland is a good place for them to come, because the Polynesians are well established here. There are plenty of shops where they can buy Polynesian food and clothing. They also have their own churches and social centers but are well accepted by the other communities. It's never easy for different cultures to live together, but I believe here in Auckland they do it very well.

Most of the Polynesians I know would not want to return to the islands, except for holidays. There's lots of opportunities and lots to do in Auckland. I have been here for seventeen years, and now think of myself as a New Zealander. I've got a good job that I've had for eleven years. I'm single, and I have a really good time. I've got no plans to change anything.

John assembles an aluminum window frame in the Auckland factory where he works.

"In the early days accidents were common"

Don Sanders is 40 years old and was born in Rotorua. He now lives in Wanganui with his wife and two children. Don is employed as an agricultural pilot, specializing in helicopter work.

Getting a helicopter license these days can be an expensive business. For a commercial license you must clock up 200 hours, the first 25 being with an instructor. At $160 ($121 U.S.) an hour for training, it helps if you can be sponsored by a company, which is how most people qualify.

There are a lot of people involved in agricultural flying in New Zealand. It's a fairly new industry, but is already a major part of the farming scene. As a helicopter

Fletcher "topdressing airplanes" being made at New Zealand Aerospace Industries Ltd in Hamilton, North Island.

pilot, most of my work is over hill country, eradicating gorse and thistle patches by spraying them with weed-killer. We also use helicopters for laying power cables, spreading seeds, delivering supplies to ships, and, a recent innovation, fire starting to clear land for pastures. We trickle ignited petroleum jelly from a drum suspended ten meters (33 feet) below the aircraft. It really is very spectacular.

We work in teams of two, a pilot and an offsider on the ground, who mixes chemicals and loads the aircraft. Weather is always the limiting factor. High winds make the flying dangerous, and hot weather causes too much spray loss through evaporation, so most of the spraying is done early in the morning. Continued bad weather causes the work to pile up, and puts pressure on the pilot to fly even when it may be unsafe to do so. During these times we are on call seven days a week, which makes planning our social and family life difficult.

It's a job that requires a lot of concentration. Spraying must be accurate, with no overlaps or missed sections – not easy when you are flying fast over rugged country, just five meters (fifteen feet) above the ground! Most pilots are on a retainer, plus a share of the profits, so we work very fast and efficiently.

Our company also operates thirty Fletcher topdressing airplanes. These are used for spreading fertilizer on pastures. They operate from a small airstrip on the farm. It's quite exciting to watch. A loading truck is sent ahead. The plane and truck come to a halt at the end of the airstrip. The hopper on the truck loads the aircraft, and as the truck backs away, the plane flicks around and takes off – all this in under twenty seconds! The plane then spreads its load, flying very low over the farmland, while the truck races off to reload its hopper from the stockpile. Both meet at the end of the strip a few minutes later. Planes are expensive to run, and this kind of efficiency is vital to stay competitive.

The Fletchers are built by New Zealand Aerospace Industries Ltd at Hamilton, in the center of the North Island. This company has pioneered the development of topdressing aircraft, and has exported them to many parts of the world. In 23 years of operating they have built 284 Fletchers, as well as many other types of specialized aircraft. There are over 8,000 farm airstrips in New Zealand, and Fletcher aircraft spread 1.2 million tonnes (1.3 million tons) of fertilizer a year from them.

In the early days accidents were common, but now with better equipment and methods, the safety record is very good. In sixteen years of flying I have had two crash landings, both without injury but with extensive damage to the aircraft. Both were caused by engine failure. The chances of this happening are very remote, so I figure I've had my ration of bad luck. Now it's up to me to avoid pilot errors.

Don sprays weed-killer on unwanted scrub from his helicopter.

"The largest known gas field in the world"

Elwyn Thomas was born in New Plymouth, a city on the western shore of the North Island. He is now working just 10 km (6 miles) from there, on a pipeline which will feed natural gas to many new industries.

From the hilltops here you can see the ocean – miles of rolling green hills, then the deep-blue water. After the Australian desert, where my last job was, the greens really look rich. Actually this area has some of the richest farmland in New Zealand.

Mount Egmont, 2,158 meters (7,808 feet) high, watches over us. Dad used to take me skiing there when I was a lad. For the last ten years, though, my home was a construction camp in Australia. When I heard of job opportunities back in New Plymouth, I thought I'd better come back and check them out.

It seems they first discovered natural gas at Kapuni, in porous sandstone, deep under the ground. Actually it was a gas/condensate mixture, so they set up a big plant to separate out the condensate, which they refined to make petrol (gasoline). Then they piped the gas to Auckland and Wellington, and many places in between, for use in homes and industry. They also produced butane, propane and liquid carbon dioxide as by-products.

All that was a big help to New Zealand, but then they discovered the Maui field, 34 km (21 miles) offshore. This one is ten times larger then Kapuni; in fact it's the largest known gas field in the world. By 1979 a huge drilling platform was in place and the gas was being piped ashore. The condensate is separated and sent to the oil refinery.

The trench of Elwyn's pipeline cuts a brown gash through the green land between Waitara and New Plymouth.

The gas has given birth to a wide range of new projects and industries. Some of it was processed at the Kapuni plant. Liquid petroleum gas was produced as an alternative to petrol for motor vehicles. Many thousands of cars and trucks have since been converted to run on this cheaper fuel. The gas is also piped to New Plymouth, where it fuels a vast 600MW electric-power generating station, the second largest station in New Zealand.

The pipeline I'm working on here will take the gas from New Plymouth to Waitara, where they are building a methanol plant. Each day, 1,200 tonnes (1,300 tons) will be produced for export, earning overseas funds. A massive synthetic petrol plant costing $760,000,000 ($577,600,000 U.S.) is also being constructed. This, along with the other schemes, will see New Zealand 50 percent self-sufficient in transport fuels by 1987. Like many other countries, New Zealand

The gas plant at Kaspuni, with the snow-capped Mount Egmont in the background.

is finding the cost of fuel a big drain on its finances, so the Maui field will be a welcome boost to the economy.

It's good to be back in my home town, especially with so much happening. The thing I missed most while I was away was New Zealand's national game — rugby football. I played rugby at school and, like many of the boys, would like to have become an All Black. They're the national team, which represents New Zealand in competitions against other countries. The name comes from their black shorts and jumper (shirt), with the silver fern emblem that all sportsmen who represent New Zealand wear.

I never made the All Blacks, but I do enjoy watching a good game. Every Saturday during the season, I join the thousands who turn out to watch the club teams; it really makes me feel I'm home again.

Facts

Capital City: Wellington.

Languages: The official language is English, but the Maoris also use their own language.

Race: After New Zealand became a British colony in 1840 great numbers of British settlers arrived, and the population is now divided into 91 percent of European origin and 8 percent indigenous Maori.

Currency: One New Zealand dollar equals 100 cents, and is worth about 76 U.S. cents.

Religion: Christian, with no single denomination being recognized by the state. Percentages are: Anglican 35 percent, Presbyterian 22 percent, Roman Catholic 16 percent, and other denominations 27 percent.

Population: In 1980 there were 3,100,100 inhabitants on the two main islands, 285,200 of these being Maori. New Zealand-born residents formed 83 percent of the population in 1976, and three-quarters of the population lives on the North Island. Only one-fifth of the population inhabit the rural areas.

Climate: The climate is temperate and moist, with no extremes of heat or cold, although it is generally warmer in the north than in the south. There are strong prevailing winds, and snow is common only in the mountains.

Government: New Zealand is an independent member of the British Commonwealth. Executive power is vested in the British monarch, and is exercised by the Governor General. Parliament consists of a House of Representatives with 92 members (including four representatives from the Maori electorate) elected for three years by universal adult suffrage. For the purposes of local government, New Zealand is divided into counties, then district councils, boroughs, and town districts. Some counties are divided into ridings. There are numerous local authorities for specific functions.

Education: Kindergartens (aged 3–4) are provided free. State education is free and compulsory between the ages of 6–15, although most children start at 5, attending primary school between the ages 5 and 11 years, intermediate education for 2 years, and secondary education up to a maximum age of 18. Secondary education covers both a broad general education and technical training. There are correspondence schools for children in remote areas and some private schools. New Zealand has 6 universities.

Housing: New Zealand enjoys a high standard of living – most families own their home, which is usually a three-bedroom bungalow on a tenth of a hectare (quarter of an acre) site. In the cities these sites are smaller and the elderly live in special apartments. The state provides rental housing for those with a low income. There are very few apartment buildings and hardly any high-rise accommodation, as land is not scarce.

Agriculture: Two-thirds of New Zealand is agricultural land. The largest freehold estates are held in the South Island. Wool, meat, butter, and cheese accounted for 52 percent of export earnings in 1979/80, with lamb and mutton alone accounting for some 12 percent of all exports. Since the U.K. joined the Common Market, New Zealand has had to increase its exports to other countries, notably in Asia. Forestry, supplying pulp and paper, is also important. Agriculture and forestry directly employ only 11.5 percent of the total labor force. Private airlines carry out aerial work, spraying crops and fertilizing pastures.

Industry: Industry accounts for 80 percent of the national income, manufacturing in particular. The main industries are food processing and canning, car assembly, transport equipment, wood and cork products, clothing, textiles, and footwear. New Zealand manufactures nearly all of its requirements of consumer goods. Import licensing restricts the entry of manufactured and processed goods from other countries, so protecting and encouraging local industry. Manufacturing industries employ 25 percent of the workforce, compared with commerce at 21 percent.

The Media: The Broadcasting Corporation of New Zealand operates two TV channels and most broadcasting stations. There are 65 medium-wave broadcasting stations and two shortwave transmitters. Both TV and radio contain some commercial material. The Press comprises 32 daily newspapers (1979 figures), with no national dailies but two main national weekly newspapers.

Glossary

bush Wild, uncultivated country.

Common Market (See E.E.C.).

condensate A liquid formed by the condensation of a gas.

conservationists People who try to preserve the natural environment.

continental plates Rigid layers of rock which make up the earth's crust.

cooperative A business unit where a group of people own the means of production and share the profits.

E.E.C. The European Economic Community, also called the Common Market. An association of several European countries which cooperate in matters of trade and economic policy.

fjord A long, narrow inlet of the sea with very high, steep sides.

geothermal power Power derived from the heat in the interior of the earth.

ice ages Periods of history when world temperatures dropped and large areas of the earth's surface were covered by ice.

intensive farm A farm on which land is used as productively as possible to give maximum yields from a limited area of land.

keeler A boat with a keel.

Maori A Polynesian people of New Zealand. A Polynesian language, the language of the Maoris.

marae A Maori meetinghouse or the land on which it stands.

pakeha The Maori name for white people.

palisading Fortifications.

probation A testing period when a person starts a new job.

pub A tavern or bar.

scow A sailing boat with a flat bottom.

sound A narrow passage of water leading inland from the sea.

tailrace A channel that carries water away from a turbine.

Index